Godmother's Journal Planner

"A godchild fills your heart with love and joy as if they were your own."

Date

_____

M T W TH F Sa Su

Top Priorities:

Appointments:

Goals For The Day:

Morning:

Afternoon:

Evening:

Notes:

"For this child, I have prayed."
1 Samuel 1:27

Date
_____

M T W TH F Sa Su

Top Priorities:

Appointments:

Goals For The Day:

Morning:

Afternoon:

Evening:

Notes:

"God has you in the palm of His hand."
Isaiah 49:16

Date

Date

_____

M T W TH F Sa Su

Top Priorities:

Appointments:

Goals For The Day:

Morning:

Afternoon:

Evening:

Notes:

"I'm a godmother. It's like a normal mother but way cooler."

Date

_____

M T W TH F Sa Su

Top Priorities:

Appointments:

Goals For The Day:

Morning:

Afternoon:

Evening:

Notes:

"A godmother always has love to give &
time to spare. A godmother is always
there."

Date

_____

M T W TH F Sa Su

Top Priorities:

Appointments:

Goals For The Day:

Morning:

Afternoon:

Evening:

Notes:

"A godmother is a gift from above. A guardian angel that was chosen with love."

Date

_____

M T W TH F Sa Su

Top Priorities:

Appointments:

Goals For The Day:

Morning:

Afternoon:

Evening:

Notes:

"You are a child of God, you are wonderfully made, dearly loved and precious in his sight". Psalm 139

Date
_____

_____

_____

_____

_____

_____

_____

_____

_____

_____

_____

_____

_____

_____

_____

_____

_____

_____

_____

_____

_____

Date
_____

M T W TH F Sa Su

Top Priorities:

Appointments:

Goals For The Day:

Morning:

Afternoon:

Evening:

Notes:

"A godmother is a special gift, one that provides the strength of family and the comfort of friendship."

Date

_____

M T W TH F Sa Su

Top Priorities:

Appointments:

Goals For The Day:

Morning:

Afternoon:

Evening:

Notes:

"Happiness is being asked to be a godmother."

Date

_____

M T W TH F Sa Su

Top Priorities:

Appointments:

Goals For The Day:

Morning:

Afternoon:

Evening:

Notes:

"Only the best aunties get promoted to Godmother."

_____

_____

_____

_____

_____

_____

_____

_____

_____

_____

_____

_____

_____

_____

_____

_____

Date

M T W TH F Sa Su

Top Priorities:

Appointments:

Goals For The Day:

Morning:

Afternoon:

Evening:

Notes:

"Godmothers are special."

Date

_____

M T W TH F Sa Su

Top Priorities:

Appointments:

Goals For The Day:

Morning:

Afternoon:

Evening:

Notes:

"Real godmothers are so much better than the fabricated, storybook kind in so many ways. I'm glad you're mine."

Date

_____

M T W TH F Sa Su

Top Priorities:

Appointments:

Goals For The Day:

Morning:

Afternoon:

Evening:

Notes:

"If you think I'm cute, you should see my godmother."

Date
_____

M T W TH F Sa Su

Top Priorities:

Appointments:

Goals For The Day:

Morning:

Afternoon:

Evening:

Notes:

"God brought you into my life and I continue to thank Him for you every day!"

Date
_____

M T W TH F Sa Su

Top Priorities:

Appointments:

Goals For The Day:

Morning:

Afternoon:

Evening:

Notes:

"My godchildren are a blessing."

Date

_____

M T W TH F Sa Su

Top Priorities:

Appointments:

Goals For The Day:

Morning:

Afternoon:

Evening:

Notes:

"He will cover you with His feathers &
under his wings you will find refuge."
Psalm 91:6

Date

_____

M T W TH F Sa Su

Top Priorities:

Appointments:

Goals For The Day:

Morning:

Afternoon:

Evening:

Notes:

"I'm cute, smart, and funny. I take after my godmother."

_____

_____

_____

_____

_____

_____

_____

_____

_____

_____

_____

_____

_____

_____

_____

_____

_____

_____

Date

M T W TH F Sa Su

Top Priorities:

Appointments:

Goals For The Day:

Morning:

Afternoon:

Evening:

Notes:

"Never forget that you are one of a kind"

Date

Date

_____

M T W TH F Sa Su

Top Priorities:

Appointments:

Goals For The Day:

Morning:

Afternoon:

Evening:

Notes:

"My Christening was made even more meaningful because of you. Thank you for being there and for the gift."

Date

_____

M T W TH F Sa Su

Top Priorities:

Appointments:

Goals For The Day:

Morning:

Afternoon:

Evening:

Notes:

"Godchild, I promise to love you, to guide you, to support you, to care for you, to encourage you, to keep you in my heart always."

Date

M T W TH F Sa Su

Top Priorities:

Appointments:

Goals For The Day:

Morning:

Afternoon:

Evening:

Notes:

"Only a godmother can give hugs like a mother, keep secrets like a sister, and share love like a friend."

Date

_____

M T W TH F Sa Su

Top Priorities:

Appointments:

Goals For The Day:

Morning:

Afternoon:

Evening:

Notes:

"May the words of my mouth & the meditations of my heart be pleasing in your sight O Lord, my rock & redeemer." Psalm 19:14

Date
_____

Date

_____

M T W TH F Sa Su

Top Priorities:

Appointments:

Goals For The Day:

Morning:

Afternoon:

Evening:

Notes:

"May the Lord give His angels charge
over you, to guide you in all your ways."
Psalm 91:11

Date

M T W TH F Sa Su

Top Priorities:

Appointments:

Goals For The Day:

Morning:

Afternoon:

Evening:

Notes:

"I need an extra pair of hands to help me learn and grow. I know that yours will be the best."

Date

_____

M T W TH F Sa Su

Top Priorities:

Appointments:

Goals For The Day:

Morning:

Afternoon:

Evening:

Notes:

"I'm a godmother. I'm kind of a big deal."

Date

_____

M T W TH F Sa Su

Top Priorities:

Appointments:

Goals For The Day:

Morning:

Afternoon:

Evening:

Notes:

"The love between a godmother and godchild is forever."

Date

_____

M T W TH F Sa Su

Top Priorities:

Appointments:

Goals For The Day:

Morning:

Afternoon:

Evening:

Notes:

"Every good and perfect gift comes from above."

James 1:17

Date

_____

M T W TH F Sa Su

Top Priorities:

Appointments:

Goals For The Day:

Morning:

Afternoon:

Evening:

Notes:

"May Jesus who loves all children, bless
your precious little one with His love and
grace on this special day and always.

Date

M T W TH F Sa Su

Top Priorities:

Appointments:

Goals For The Day:

Morning:

Afternoon:

Evening:

Notes:

"It means so much being a Godparent to a godchild as special as you."

_____

_____

_____

_____

_____

_____

_____

_____

_____

_____

_____

_____

_____

_____

_____

_____

Date

M T W TH F Sa Su

Top Priorities:

Appointments:

Goals For The Day:

Morning:

Afternoon:

Evening:

Notes:

"Godmother: a divinely chosen guardian."

Date

_____

M T W TH F Sa Su

Top Priorities:

Appointments:

Goals For The Day:

Morning:

Afternoon:

Evening:

Notes:

"A godmother watches over your
spiritual path."

Date

_____

M T W TH F Sa Su

Top Priorities:

Appointments:

Goals For The Day:

Morning:

Afternoon:

Evening:

Notes:

"She is a protector that will be a constant in your life. She was chosen particularly for you."

Date

_____

M T W TH F Sa Su

Top Priorities:

Appointments:

Goals For The Day:

Morning:

Afternoon:

Evening:

Notes:

"I get my awesomeness from my godmother."

Date
_____

_____

_____

_____

_____

_____

_____

_____

_____

_____

_____

_____

_____

_____

_____

_____

_____

_____

_____

Date

_____

M T W TH F Sa Su

Top Priorities:

Appointments:

Goals For The Day:

Morning:

Afternoon:

Evening:

Notes:

"Sometimes the littlest things take up the most room in your heart."
Winnie the Pooh

Date
_____

Date
_____

M T W TH F Sa Su

Top Priorities:

Appointments:

Goals For The Day:

Morning:

Afternoon:

Evening:

Notes:

"And the child grew and became strong in spirit." Luke 1:80

_____

_____

_____

_____

_____

_____

_____

_____

_____

_____

_____

_____

_____

_____

_____

_____

Date

M T W TH F Sa Su

Top Priorities:

Appointments:

Goals For The Day:

Morning:

Afternoon:

Evening:

Notes:

"May you always know my little one you were wished for, longed for, prayed for, and wanted."

Date

_____

M T W TH F Sa Su

Top Priorities:

Appointments:

Goals For The Day:

Morning:

Afternoon:

Evening:

Notes:

"Godparents are a blessing of love &
guidance. A special gift from heaven
above."

Date

_____

M T W TH F Sa Su

Top Priorities:

Appointments:

Goals For The Day:

Morning:

Afternoon:

Evening:

Notes:

"Godparents are a blessing of love & guidance. A special gift from heaven above."

Date

_____

M T W TH F Sa Su

Top Priorities:

Appointments:

Goals For The Day:

Morning:

Afternoon:

Evening:

Notes:

"Children are a gift from the Lord; they are a reward from Him."
Psalm 127:3

_____

_____

_____

_____

_____

_____

_____

_____

_____

_____

_____

_____

_____

_____

_____

_____

_____

_____

_____

Date

_____

M T W TH F Sa Su

Top Priorities:

Appointments:

Goals For The Day:

Morning:

Afternoon:

Evening:

Notes:

"Godmother is a gift sent from above, bringing kisses, hugs, and never ending love."

Date

M T W TH F Sa Su

Top Priorities:

Appointments:

Goals For The Day:

Morning:

Afternoon:

Evening:

Notes:

"Godmother, a special person who can guide and mentor."

Date

_____

M T W TH F Sa Su

Top Priorities:

Appointments:

Goals For The Day:

Morning:

Afternoon:

Evening:

Notes:

"Because I know you'll love me. Because
I know you'll care. Because I know
you'll always be there."

Date

_____

M T W TH F Sa Su

Top Priorities:

Appointments:

Goals For The Day:

Morning:

Afternoon:

Evening:

Notes:

"Godmothers have ears that truly listen, arms that always hold, a love that's never ending, and a heart made of gold."

Date

_____

M T W TH F Sa Su

Top Priorities:

Appointments:

Goals For The Day:

Morning:

Afternoon:

Evening:

Notes:

"You are loved beyond measure."
Romans 8: 38–39

Date

_____

M T W TH F Sa Su

Top Priorities:

Appointments:

Goals For The Day:

Morning:

Afternoon:

Evening:

Notes:

"How amazing it is to find someone who wants to hear about all the things that go on in your head." Nina LaCour

Date

_____

M T W TH F Sa Su

Top Priorities:

Appointments:

Goals For The Day:

Morning:

Afternoon:

Evening:

Notes:

"How amazing it is to find someone who wants to hear about all the things that go on in your head." Nina LaCour

Date

_____

M T W TH F Sa Su

Top Priorities:

Appointments:

Goals For The Day:

Morning:

Afternoon:

Evening:

Notes:

Notes

Notes

Notes

Notes

Notes

Notes

Notes

www.ingramcontent.com/pod-product-compliance
Lightning Source LLC
Chambersburg PA
CBHW051033030426
42336CB00015B/2853